Yorkshire Customs

60p

Yorkshire Customs

Traditions and Folk Lore of Old Yorkshire

by

Arnold Crowther

Dalesman Books
1974

The Dalesman Publishing Company Ltd.,
Clapham (via Lancaster), North Yorkshire.

First published 1974

ISBN: 0 85206 250 8

Printed in Great Britain by
Galava Printing Co. Ltd., Hallam Road, Nelson, Lancashire

Contents

The front cover painting of the Ripon horn-blower is by Bruce Danz.

The drawings in the text are by the author, and by Bernard Fearley (page 27), M. Barringer (page 28), G. Ragland Phillips (pages 35 and 62), Joseph Appleyard (page 40), E. Gower (page 56), Stanley Bond (page 63), and B. Waters (page 65).

Preface

YORKSHIRE has an almost inexhaustible store of customs, tradition and folk lore stemming from almost every town, village, mountain, dale and moor. Indeed, one wonders if every house not more than a few decades old has not a story hidden somewhere among its stones. So a collection like this can only dip into that richness and pick at random among items that are known and familiar to many and others that have been forgotten and are worth re-telling.

The chapters in this book can be read in several ways. They can be entertaining footnotes to north-country history and topography. The customs and traditions of a land can illuminate its true history with a light of their own which throws into strong relief aspects of bygone life—aspects which might otherwise have been overlooked or unknown. A county which forgets its past is poor indeed, and this little collection may remind us of Yorkshire's rich and varied store.

1. Yorkshire Tykes and their Tales

A TRAVELLER once remarked that the British Isles comprised five distinct races — the English, the Scots, the Irish, the Welsh and the Yorkshire "tykes". This latter expression is inoffensively employed within and outside the county, although no one seems to know from whence the nickname arose or whether it was viewed with complacency or otherwise. We certainly find a "tyke" rather rudely described by an authority in 1363 as "dog, mongrel; hence, a clodhopper, a churl, a mean snarling rascal; especially a Yorkshireman". This 14th century date gives some idea of the antiquity of this strange term, which is definitely employed nowadays in a complimentary manner irrespective of whatever our "Dictionaries of Slang and Colloquial English" may suggest to the contrary.

It must be understood, furthermore, that the Yorkshireman certainly possesses some very distinct characteristics. Perhaps the most outstanding trait is that of caution. Even in this age of speed and quick decisions, the genuine "tyke" does not believe in dashing at things. It is not surprising that, while agreeing upon his frank heartiness and delightful hospitality, many wits have united to subject his shrewdness to ridicule. "A Yorkshireman's Compliment" is described in our "Slang Dictionary" as something that is useless to the giver and not wanted by the receiver. "Yorkshire Estates" are those which will only arrive when money is forthcoming with which to purchase them. "A Yorkshire Bite" is "a specially cute piece of over-reaching, entrapping one into a profitless bargain"; while, according to a book in the Lancashire dialect (1757), the phrase "To come Yorkshire over any person" is "to cheat or cozen him" and that "proverbial over-reaching of the rustics there originally gave rise to that expression". It is fortunate that the Yorkshireman has a keen sense of humour and is not easily upset by ridicule, irony or invective, or he would be particularly disturbed by the semi-humorous coat-of-arms with which his county has traditionally been invested.

Yorkshire has long been one of the few English places to possess its own semi-satirical armorial bearings. In these are

A tykes' mug showing the traditional
Yorkshire coat-of-arms.

usually portrayed in its quartings a flea, a fly and a flitch of
bacon, which are purposed to depict the characteristic traits of
those indigenous to the soil. One of the earliest of these coat-of-
arms was designed in 1818 by Thomas Tegg of Cheapside,
London. In heraldic language there was displayed on a shield a
ham, flanked by a flea, a fly and at the base, a magpie. A horse's
head with its neck in a halter was the crest. Supports were
dexter, a huntsman; sinister, a groom. Above the motto were two
foxes' brushes. There was a rigmarole which ran: "A Tyke and
a fly, sir, 'tis very well known, will drink with all comers, from
anyone's glass; and a Tyke, like a flea, sir, will bite friend or
foe; and a magpie and Tyke, with lad, sir or lass, will chatter
all day; while a Tyke, like a flitch, is no good at all till hanged,
sir, he be." So the Tyke's coat-of-arms for ages had been a
magpie, a flitch, a flea, or, to put it together in cynical rhyme:

A flea will bite who ivver it can—
An' so, my lads will a Yorkshireman;
A fly will sup with Dick, Tom or Dan—
An' so begow will a Yorkshireman!
A magpie can talk for a terrible span—
An' so an' all, can a Yorkshireman;
A flitch is no good till it's hung, ye'll agree—
No more is a Yorkshireman, don't ye see.

The tyke's motto is:

> *See all, hear all, say nowt,*
> *Eat all, sup all, pay nowt;*
> *And if tha does owt for nowt,*
> *Allus do it for thisen.*

An equally well-known old Yorkshire toast runs: "Here's tiv us. May we nivver want nowt, no 'en on us, all on us, nor me nawther. Here's health to ma wife's husband — tak hod an' sup, lad."

2. The Language of Hearth and Home

DIALECTS are admittedly a survival of our original heritage of speech — simple in form and expression of thought — and subject in a far less degree to the changes in pronunciation and idiom that afflict or illuminate our educated speech. It cannot be denied that there is a robustness in the dialect of Yorkshire, both in word and speech, which is only too often absent from modern English. The pronunciation in the dialect has, in fact, been preserved in all its purity from Anglo-Saxon times and from Norse occupation. In many cases, the Yorkshire dialect is simply a more phonetic way of pronunciation. For instance, a Yorkshire-man pronounces such words as father, warm and warn according to their spelling, i.e. in the same way as gather, farm and darn.

One must remember that Yorkshire is the most Danish part of England. "Stadhr", for instance, is the Icelandic name for "landing-stage" and it is still preserved in "Staithes". There is no definite article in east Yorkshire no doubt because in the Scandinavian language the definite article was a suffix, "en" or "et" according to gender. The public house sign of *The Pig and Whistle* still recalls the Scandinavian "Pige og Wassail", i.e. "Women and Wine". The expression "Hear tell" is obviously from the Norwegian "Yeg har hord tale" (I have heard talk or tell) and the Norwegian "En Dearlig dg" was just the Yorkshire for "a dowly day".

Walter Haigh's glossary of the Dialect of the Huddersfield district is a real mine of interest. To the son's enquiry of what the dinner was to consist, the father replied: "Lean wife roasted, and t' ruin o' man for sauce", which means "roasted spare-rib of pork and apple sauce". An immoral woman, in Yorkshire, is called a "besom". In bygone days, mothers were careful to prevent their daughters from stepping over a broom, but some spiteful people sometimes laid one where the girl would walk over it by accident.

There is a Yorkshire saying, "As tight as owd Dick's hatband, 'at went twice rahnd and then wouldn't tie". "Ez thrang ez a woman's tongue" is another Yorkshire simile. "He will be hanged for leaving his liquor, like the saddler of Bawtry" is an expression applied to a man who leaves his friends too early at a convivial meeting. It is explained as follows. Between the city of York and the place of execution there was an inn called the *Gallow's House,* at which the procession with condemned people was accustomed to stop for a drink. The saddler in question refused this refreshment and hastened to execution. Too late a reprieve arrived which would have saved his life if he had only waited as usual at the inn.

Other quaint similes include: "As stupid as a pot mule"; "A mouth like a parish oven"; "Like t' parson's white hen, that never laid away"; "Lazy as Ludlam's dog, that leaned his head against a wall to bark". Sheffield claims that the dog in question was called Bingo and was a guardian of the wine-bins belonging to old Lulam (not Ludlam) who kept an alehouse about 1787 in Scotland Street.

Another Yorkshire saying suggests that "It is better to be at the baiting of a bear than the singing of a Mass". This is said to date from the year 1520 when, on the first Sunday in April, a bear was being baited at the same time the Mass was being sung. Only 55 people attended the Mass at St. Mary's church, Beverley, and the chancel fell and killed them all. The thousand and odd who watched the bear being baited lived.

Other sayings and proverbs include: "It's a poor hedge that hasn't a bit of shelter"; "Good luck gives to some more than what they ought to have but never more than what they want"; "You will have to crack the shells before you can count the kernels" (You will have to do your work before you can count your wages); "Never judge the blade by the heft"; "It's a bag of moonshine" (nonsense); "It's not oft t' kitten brings t' owd cat a mouse"; "It's a good horse that never stumbles and a good wife that never grumbles"; "There's nowt lost where they keep a pig"; "It's a bad bargain that both sides rue".

Anyone who has heard a Yorkshire moorland shepherd counting his sheep has had a fortunate experience. It is a relic of the past that has withstood the march of civilisation: "Yain, tain, eddero, peddero, pitts, tayter, later, overro, coverro, dix, yain-dix, tain-dix, eddero-dix, peddero-dix, bumfit, yain-o-bumfit, tain-o-bumfit, eddero-bumfit, peddero-bumfit, jiggit." In the Ribblesdale area the counting, which points to a common Celtic origin, runs: "Aen, taen, tethera, fethera, phubs, aayther, layather, quoather, quaatha-dugs, aena-dugs, taena-dugs, tethera-dugs, fethera-dugs, buon, aena-buon, taena-buon, tethera-buon, fethera-buon."

Yorkshire folk of yore used the word "scratch" for a type of sofa. It appears to be a corruption of "cratch" which means an open framework, a rack, a manger. In the original manuscript of "Christians Awake", John Byron used the words: "A cratch contains the Holy Babe Divine".

A milk-and-water individual was described as, "He's nayther gut ner gall". "They doan't put up their hosses togither" described two friends who had quarrelled. As to the weather, we find the following obsolete expressions: "It's a March hig" (passing hurricane); "Hen-scrattins, and filly tails i' t' sky" (white clouds denoting wind or rain). If rain fell, an old Yorkshireman would say it was a "Pelsy" or a "Pash" or, in the case of small rain, it was "Deggy" or "Mislin". As he poured out a glass of liquor for a friend, he would say: "A sup o' gin t' warm t' cockles o' thi heart", and they would drink until one or the other was "Fair rossined".

From the 1870s until the beginning of the present century, dialect almanacs were a peculiar feature of West Riding life. They came into being with the spread of education when books were still too expensive to be bought by the working classes. Their rise to popularity and phenomenal circulation came when the puns and predictions were read by the yellow gleam of candles and paraffin lamps. Their decline came as the cost of books lessened, and as the interest in dialect waned. They were paper bound and consisted of from twenty to forty pages, printed on inferior paper. Many of the covers were printed in two colours, usually red and yellow, and bearing an illustration in which there was almost certainly a Churchwarden pipe in evidence. These little books cost from one penny to sixpence, and apart from notes of local history of the past year, they were saturated with the pawky humour of the Riding in dialect.

The most famous and longest-lived of these dialect almanacs was John Hartley's *Clock Almanac* which had for many years a circulation of about 75,000. It was published from 1864 until 1936. Here are some of the others: *Bob Stubbs' Almanac* (1907-29); *Th' Beacon* (Halifax, 1873-76); *T' Leeds Loiners' Comic Olmenac* (1873-82); *Nidderdale Olminac and Ivverybodd's Kalinder* (1868-76); *Nidderdill Comic Casket* (1877-80); *Pudsey Almanac* (1858-74); *Tommy Toddler's Comic Almanac fur all t' Foak i' Leeds and raand abaht* (1863-75); *Yorkshireman's Comic Annual incorporating Saunterer's Satchell* (1882-95); *Tyke's Own Almanac* (1924).

Yorkshire has some decidedly curious place names. There is the scriptural Nineveh, and there is also a hamlet named Mount Tabor, near Halifax. An ordnance map will reveal Zion Hill and Salem Chapel, and also three farms called Noah's Ark. One of the strangest villages must be that of Hades, near Holmfirth. It is a tiny cluster of houses mainly occupied by farm workers which completely belies its name for it is situated amid delightful moorland scenery, nestling in the hillside, with a tree-surrounded reservoir below. It is said that some years ago the occupiers of the farm there left because they found Hades too cold.

A strange custom in bygone Yorkshire was the use of "by-names", and, although they are rarely employed nowadays, they are not unknown in smaller places. According to a correspondent in the *York Weekly Post* for 11th July, 1936, an inquiry was made in the vicinity of Slaithwaite for a man named Thomas Clay. The woman looked bewildered, then something seemed to "ring a bell": "Ee, why mister, I do believe it's yar owd man yor wantin'. But I'd fair forgotten they called him Clay. We ne'er call him nowt nobbut Tom o' Salls." Sall, of course, was his mother's name. If her father's name chanced to be Bob, his own could easily have been Tom o' Salls o' Bobs.

There are several old Yorkshire customs concerning names. Before a baby is nine days old, it is considered wise to decide upon its name, and once a name is suggested it must not be changed. If either of the parents should happen to say, "We will call it so-and-so", it is thought unwise to make any alteration for otherwise it is thought the child will grow up as a liar and will probably have to assume several aliases before death. In Cleveland, it was said that such a proceeding "can end with nowt bud harm" but it was never said in what form the harm would come.

There is a legend in Wensleydale to the effect that a soul was once permitted to view the body it would shortly tenant and, on its return to the land of spirits, it gave a full description of the name by which it would be known on earth. It was later dismayed, on being carried to the font, to discover that it was being christened by another name. For a time it was sorely troubled. What could it do? There was only one course open, it must hurry back to the spirit-land and clear itself from an apparent untruth. In order to do this, it had to free itself from the body. This caused the baby to die. Because of this legend, it is considered extremely bad luck to decide on the child's name before it is born, and then to change it afterwards.

3. Characters of Old Yorkshire

IN *Yorkshire Longevity* by W. Grange (1864) the names of 248
centenarians are given. The list includes Jonathan Hartop, of
Aldborough, who died in 1791, aged 138. He remembered the
Great Fire of London in 1666, knew the poet Milton and possessed
a portrait of Cromwell. On Christmas day, 1789, he walked nine
miles to dine with one of his grandchildren.

John Phillips, of Thorne, apparently lived under eight monarchs
as well as the Protectorate of Cromwell and reached 117 years.
W. White's *History, Gazette and Directory of the West Riding*
(1839) says that George Firton, of Oxnop Hall, who died at the
age of 125, was a noted fox hunter and followed the chase on
horseback until after he was 80, and after that it was his custom
to attend the "breaking cover" — the unkennelling of the fox —
in his chair until he reached his hundredth year. A woman of
107, who died near Wakefield, left 156 descendants, but this
record was broken by a Hunslet centenarian who left 258, and
nearly a hundred of them attended her funeral.

Many people still believe that Henry Jenkins could never have
reached the recorded age of 169, but Mrs. Anne Saville, who
lived at Bolton (where the aged patriarch is buried) at the time
of the restoration of King Charles II, fathomed the history of
Yorkshire's oldest inhabitant and was entirely satisfied. He
apparently remembered King Henry VIII and the battle of
Flodden Field in 1513. Dayes, the painter and tutor of Turner
and Girtin, who made a pedestrian excursion of Yorkshire in
1803, noted that Henry Jenkins followed the employment of
fisherman for 140 years, and that when he had reached the age
of 160 he used to bind sheafs of corn for farmers. Three queens
— Anne Boleyn, Catherine Howard and Mary Queen of Scots —
were beheaded in his time. He is said to have swum the river
Swale when he was over one hundred years old. His epitaph, at
Bolton, reads:

"Blush not marble to rescue from oblivion the memory of
Henry Jenkins, a person of obscure birth, but of a life truly
memorable. For he was enriched with the goods of Nature, if
not with fortune, and happy in the duration, if not variety of his

enjoyments. And though the partial world despised and disregarded his lot and humble state, the equal Eye of Providence beheld and blessed it with a patriarch's health and length of days. To teach mistaken man these blessings are entail'd on temperance, a life of labour and a mind at ease. He lived to the amazing age of 169. He was interred here December 6, 1670 and had justice done to his memory, 1743."

It was said that only the excitement of having to travel to York as witness in a case concerning the Vicar of Catterick prevented him from living to a "really ripe old age". Whatever may be the truth of this matter, a story is told of a certain attorney in quest of evidence who journeyed to Ellerton-upon-Swale. There he saw in the garden of a cottage a feeble, white haired man who, when questioned, said: "Ah deant knaw owt aboot it. Gang yer ways int' t' hoose, an' ask mi fayther; he'll 'appen tell ya". Upon doing this, the man-of-the-law found a wreck of humanity who with difficulty explained that his memory was gone, but his "fadder at t' back o' t' hoose, chopping sticks could tell ya all aboot it". Marvelling still more, the lawyer found the patriarch hale and hearty at the age of 166 and far more vigorous than his grandson. He was able to satisfy the legal gentleman and enabled him to win the case.

Although some of Yorkshire's giants may have been legendary characters, it is certain that in William Beaucless we get an authentic one. This schoolmaster at Hutton is reported in the *Gentleman's Magazine* of 1798 to have been 7ft 8ins in height. William Bradley of Market Weighton was 7ft 9ins in height, and his coffin, in 1820, had to measure 9ft by 3ft. Robert Hales, landlord of the *Burgoyne Arms,* Sheffield, had a height of 7ft 6ins and a weight of 452lbs when he died on 22nd November, 1863. James Dunwell, of Brokenfoot, near Harrogate, weighed over 40 stones. When he died on 28th August, 1829, in his 25th year, he was claimed to be the fattest man in England.

The Rev. Joseph Coltman of Beverley was weighed at the Foundry some four years before his death in 1837, and turned the scales at 45 stones. Isaac Butterfield of Keighley, a baby who died in February 1783, measured 3ft in height and weighed 8 stones. One of Yorkshire's fattest women was Isabella Cryer. She came from Leeds and measured 3 yards round her waist, and weighed 40 stones. She was carried to her last resting place by ten men.

Charles Bosville, King of the Yorkshire Gipsies, died in 1708. He was buried at Rossington, Doncaster. Among the various ceremonies enacted was the pouring of a flagon of ale over his grave. This custom was repeated annually for many years. Jemmy Hirst, a wealthy "oddity", died in 1829 at the age of ninety-one. He had his coffin already made, and at his funeral the procession

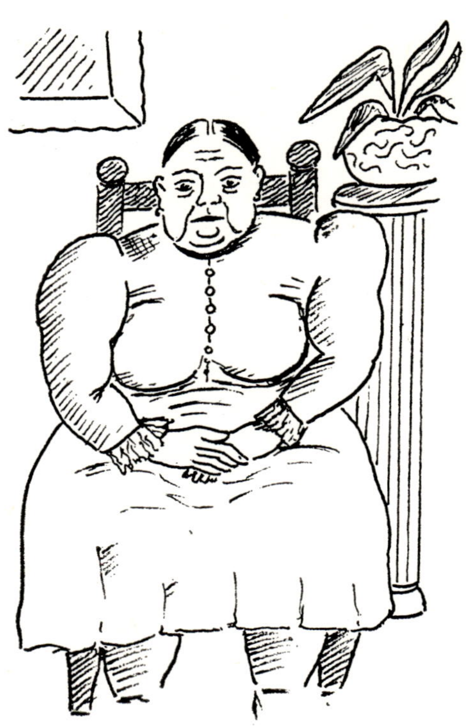

Isabella Cryer of Leeds, who at 40 stones was one of Yorkshire's fattest women.

included gentry and farmers on horseback, a piper from Aberdeen, six old maids and two men carrying the coffin and six more old maids bearing the pall. The piper and a fiddler afterwards played, "Ower the hills and far awa'".

Many stories are told about a peculiarly uncouth creature that used to visit the villages of Airedale and Wharfedale just over one hundred years ago. His appearance was anything but prepossessing. His wild eyes and unkempt locks made him appear more like a beast than a man. He dressed in rags which were kept in place by pieces of string. Almost bent double, and with a stick in each hand, he hobbled through Bingley, Shipley, Otley and other places in the neighbourhood, and made his living by begging coppers from the villagers. Old Job Senior, as he was called, was as much a novelty to the locals as the fat woman or six-legged sheep at a fair. It was said that a love disappointment had

**Old Job Senior, a well-known hermit
in Airedale and Wharfedale villages.**

caused him to lead the life of a hermit. The truth was that Job
had never been particularly fond of work, and when he was about
sixty he proposed marriage to an old widow named Mary Barrett.
She believed that he was really in love with her, and in due time
they were wedded at Otley church. His wife lived for six years
after their wedding, and there was a great deal of unpleasantness
when she died and a nephew claimed the cottage. Job died at
the age of 77, friendless and unmourned. He was buried in Burley
churchyard.

Another Yorkshire eccentric was Charles Waterton, who was
born at Walton Hall, Wakefield, in 1782. Although he had
considerable wealth he wore neither stockings nor shoes and very
little clothing when he went out, and even slept at night in an
open hammock in the forest. He knew no fear, and on one
occasion he climbed to the top of St. Peter's in Rome, and then
climbed thirteen feet higher than the cross and left his gloves
on the top of the lightning conductor. At the special command
of the Pope he had to repeat the performance to bring the gloves

down again. From his childhood days, Charles Waterton showed a keen interest in natural history, and was always a lover of birds and animals. The only animal he detested was the rat, and during his College days he developed considerable ability in curtailing the career of the rats that swarmed through the ancient mansions. Even the wily fox found sanctuary in his park, and all fur and feathered creatures found a haven of refuge in his extensive grounds. He even had special nests built in the trees for owls.

Charles Waterton, the eccentric squire of Walton Hall near Wakefield (drawn from a portrait in the National Portrait Gallery).

Lumley Kettlewell, who was born in 1751 and resided for many years at Clemonthorpe, was one of the oddest of Yorkshire's "characters". The son of a wealthy farmer, his fortune, manners and education unquestionably made him a gentleman in every respect, but for some unaccountable reason he renounced in middle age the comforts of the world and became a hermit. He wore the most incongruous garments. Sometimes he would wear a fur cap with full evening-dress jacket and top boots; at other times he appeared in a top-hat with a coat of oilskin, finished off with the torn remains of black silk stockings. No human being was allowed to enter his mansion, and the front door was always barricaded. He used to climb a ladder to enter a small aperture which had once been a window. He slept in an old crate filled with hay, while his diet appears to have consisted of the most uninviting things such as cocks' heads with their wattles and combs baked in a pudding of bran and treacle. Vinegar and water was his usual beverage. He left his money about on window sills and chairs, and banknotes were often

Lumley Kettlewell, a "gentleman hermit" who barricaded himself off from the outside world and climbed a ladder in order to sleep in a crate.

eaten by rats. He finally died of personal neglect and privation in obscure lodgings.

Margaret Warburton, an unmarried lady of good family stock, lived at Scarborough. She possessed a fortune of £200,000 and her charitable work was extensive, although she always said that if the recipient ever disclosed her good deed, that person would never receive another penny from her. She earned the nickname of Pennyworth from her custom of sending for a pennyworth of strawberries and a pennyworth of cream at a time, always paying cash, as she had an aversion to tradesmen's bills. She died in 1791 at the age of 103.

James Hirst was another original fellow. He lived in the village of Rawcliffe when George III was king. As a boy, Jimmy rode his father's pigs and trained them to jump. As a man, he mounted bulls and rode with the hounds on his favourite bull-calf Jupiter. He invented various gadgets for cutting straw, chopping turnips, etc., but the device that made him famous was the wickerwork palanquin he built for his own accommodation, to which he harnessed four Andalusian mules. The curiosity of George III was tickled by the various accounts he had heard of this eccentric, and he sent a Royal Command for the homely Yorkshireman to visit him. Mr. Hirst was in no hurry to obey the king's command, but at last he set off to London in his strange wickerwork carriage. Crowds of people gathered to see him all along the route, and when he reached the capital the mules had great difficulty in getting along at all for the crush.

James Hirst of Rawcliffe rode to hounds on his favourite bull-calf, Jupiter.

The following morning he proceeded to the Palace, and when he was presented to the king he grasped him by the hand and said: "Eh, I'm glad to see thee such a plain owd chap. If thou ever comes to Rawcliffe step in and give me a visit. I can give thee some rare good wine, or a sup of brandy and water at any time." When he left the Palace he escorted the king and his courtiers to where his quaint vehicle was standing, and showed them that the contrivance which held his supply of wine was empty. The king had it filled from his own wine cellars. When James got back to Rawcliffe, he indulged himself in bull-baiting, cock-fighting, hunting and bear-baiting. One day, when putting his bull-mount, Jupiter, at a fence, the beast fell and broke his master's leg. Thereupon Hirst, fertile as ever in ingenuity, built an appliance for his wounded leg, by which a string fixed to a hook in the ceiling supported his limb, raising it to whatever height he required. He finally invented his own coffin which had folding doors, glass panels and an arrangement for ringing a bell.

There have been numerous religious fanatics, but James Nayler was actually hailed as the Messiah. He was born in 1616 at East Ardsley and served as a Quartermaster in the Parliamentary Army. In 1651 he was converted by George Fox and became a preacher. He won many converts in the South and the Midlands, and it was said that on one occasion he raised a woman from the dead. This caused him to be charged with blasphemy and he was sent to prison as a vagrant. As his features bore a near resemblance to the common pictures of Our Lord, he assumed the character of the Messiah and was acknowledged as such by his deluded followers. He effected to heal the sick and raise the dead, and entered triumphantly into Bristol, attended by his followers who strewed leaves and branches before him. He was pilloried, burnt through the tongue, and branded with a "B" on his forehead for blasphemy, and was moreover sentenced to be whipped and confined to hard labour. Strangely enough, Nayler never claimed to be the Messiah or anything else, but he never tried to stop his followers hailing him as such.

The Rev. John Alcock, Rector of Burnsall, was a born wit and some of his jests were very amusing. He surprised his congregation on one occasion by reading about four verses of the first chapter of St. Matthew and then saying: "And so on to the end of the chapter — here endeth the second lesson." Once, on taking out his sermon, he discovered that a brother wag had unstitched the leaves and replaced them higgledy-piggledy. The minister explained what had occurred and said: "I have no time to put the leaves in their proper order. I shall read it as I find it. You can put it together when you get home."

The Rev. Daniel Chapman, who was a Wesleyan minister in Yorkshire, was noted for using long words in ordinary conversation. He used to travel to his appointments by pony and trap. On one occasion, when he arrived at his destination, he said to the ostler: "Extricate the quadruped from the vehicle; stabulate and apportion him an adequate supply of nutritiousaliment, and, when the solar orb shall again illuminate the eastern horizon, I will reward your hospitality with the needful pecuniary advantage." The ostler, evidently not understanding, called to his master: "Heigh, mastor, here's a Frenchman. See what he wants!"

About ninety years ago, the Rector of Thornhill was a witty and eccentric man named Toor, who was often invited to dine with the squire, as much noted for his meanness as for his fondness of rabbits. To this dish the Rev. H. Toor strongly objected, and when asked on the last occasion to say grace he delivered the following:

> "Rabbits hot and rabbits cold,
> Rabbits young and rabbits old,
> Rabbits tender, rabbits tough,
> We thank the Lord we've had enough."

4. Yorkshire Folk Rhymes

MANY places in Yorkshire have old rhymes connected with them. Even the remains of the Druidical circle on Addleborough Hill is mentioned in the following couplet:

Druid, Roman, Scandinavia,
Stone raise on Addleboro'.

Not all rhymes were complimentary to the places, and Beswick, near Beverley, must have been unpopular by the poet who wrote this verse:

A thatched church, a wooden steeple,
A drunken parson and wicked people.

Similar rhymes were written about Raskel in North Yorkshire, and Market Weighton:

A wooden church, a wooden steeple,
Rascally church, rascally people.
Market Weighton, Robert Leighton,
A brick church, a wooden steeple,
A drunken priest and wicked people.

Robert Leighton was a well-known local farmer. It is not known whether these three verses were written by the same person, but it is most probable that local wits altered the original verse to apply to their own villages.

When clouds gathered on the top of well-known hills, it often denoted a coming storm, and a couplet to this effect is written about Rawdon Billing:

When Billing Hill puts on its cap
Calverley mill will get a slap.

One couplet is said to describe the people of various places:

(To sheddle, in the Leeds dialect, is to swindle.)

Richard Tempest, who owned Bolling Hall, near Bradford, was
a great gambler, and according to legend he staked and lost the
Hall at a game of cards. During the deal, he exclaimed:

Now ace, duce, and tray,
Or farewell Bolling Hall for ever and aye.

Calverley Hall is said to be haunted by the ghost of Walter
Calverley, who on 23rd April 1604 murdered several of his
children by stabbing them with a dagger. For this crime he was
pressed to death at York Castle. The writer of an article in a
Bradford paper of 1874 described how, in his boyhood days, he
assisted in an invocation to raise the ghost of the old murderous
squire. The modus operandi was as follows:

"About a dozen of the scholars having leisure, and fired with
the imaginative spirit, used to assemble after school hours close
to the venerable Church of Calverley, and then put their hats
and caps down on the ground, in a pyramidal form. Then taking
hold of each other's hands they formed a 'magic circle', holding
firmly together, and making use of an old refrain:

Old Calverley, old Calverley, I have thee by the ear,
I'll cut thee into collops, unless thee appear.

While this incantation was going on, crumbs of bread (saved
from their dinner) and mixed with pins, were strewn on the
ground, the meanwhile the lads tramped round in a circle with
heavy tread. Some of the more venturesome boys had to go
round to each of the church doors, and whistle aloud through
the keyhole, repeating the magical couplet which their comrades
in the circle were chanting. At this culminating point a pale and
ghostly figure was expected to appear, and on one occasion,
some such apparition does seem to have issued forth, apparently
from the church. The lads in their terrified haste to avoid the
ghost's fearful grasp, scampered off as fast as their legs would
carry them, leaving their hats and caps scattered about the
ground as legitimate spoil for old Calverley."

At Richmond Castle, King Arthur and his knights are said to
lie spellbound under the roots of the great tower. A certain
Potter Thompson was once led into the vault and saw the king
and his knights, and on a table were placed a horn and sword.

Richmond Castle viewed from the river Swale. King Arthur and his knights are said to lie spellbound under the roots of the great tower of the castle.

He began to draw the sword, but as the sleepers stirred he became frightened and dropped it. A voice exclaimed:

Potter, Potter Thompson,
If thou hadst either drawn
The sword, or blown the horn,
Thou'dst been the luckiest man that ever yet was born.

Near Bainbridge in Wensleydale is Semerwater, a lake of one hundred and five acres with a wood round its shores. There is a tradition that a large town once stood on this site, and an old man sought alms from house to house. He received nothing until he came to a cottage on the outskirts, where he was given food and lodgings for the night. The following day he departed and, looking back on the town, he exclaimed:

Semerwater is associated with one of Yorkshire's best-known legends. A beggar was refused food at the village here, and so uttered a curse which caused the lake to rise and drown the inhabitants.

Simmer water rise, Simmer water sink,
And swallow all the town
Save yon li'le house
Where they gave me meat and drink.

The water rose and all perished save the inhabitants of the li'le house.

The tradition of Osmotherley refers to a woman who had an only son called Os, or Oscar. Strolling out one day with her child they met a party of gipsies who offered to tell the boy's fortune. The mother agreed, and to her astonishment and grief they predicted the child would be drowned. To prevent this, the woman bought some ground and had a house built on top of a high hill, where the two lived in peace and seclusion. One fine summer day after a long walk they became fatigued, lay down on the ground to rest and fell asleep. While they were sleeping, a spring rose and caused such an inundation that the two of them found a watery grave. After this had happened, the people living in the neighbourhood named it Os-by-his-mother-lay, which became corrupted into Osmotherley.

Some other Yorkshire folk rhymes are detailed below:

Wharfe is clear and in the Aire lithe,
Where the Aire drowns one, Wharfe drowns five.

*   *   *

Winkabank and Templebrough
Will buy all England through and through.

Winkabank, now called Wincobank, is near Sheffield, and has a wooded hill which contains the remains of an ancient camp. Templebrough stands between the Rother and the Don, about a quarter of a mile from the place where the two rivers meet. Near here there was believed to have been a temple to the old god Thor, as there is a pool called Jordon dam, which name appears to be composed of Jor, one of the names of the god Thor, and Don, the name of the river.

The tradition of Osmotherley involves fortune-telling and subsequent grief.

London streets shall run with blood,
And at last shall sink,
So that it shall be fulfill'd
That Lincoln was, London is, and York shall be
The finest city of the three.

(This was one of the prophecies of Nixon, the Cheshire Merlin. It is also a fact that the Londoners are very concerned about the excessive rising of the river Thames.)

*   *   *

Castleford women must needs be fair,
Because they wash both in Calder and Aire.

(Castleford is an old Roman station at the junction of the two West Riding rivers, where the Calder ceases.)

*   *   *

The Lord of Dacres
Was slain in North Acres.

(At the battle of Towton, the Lancastrian Lord Dacres was shot in a field called Nor Acres, by a boy from a "burtre" (elder tree).)

*   *   *

When Dighton is pulled down,
Hull shall become a greater town.

(Dighton, a small town near Hull, was almost pulled down at the time of the Civil War, and remained a shambles for many years.)

*   *   *

The Doncaster Mayor he sits in his chair,
The Mills they merrily go;
His nose doth shine with drinking wine,
And the gout is in his great toe.

(The profits of the town mills, near the bridge over the Don, were anciently assigned for special expenses of the Mayor.)

*   *   *

The shelving, slimy river Dun (Don)
Each year a daughter or a son. (drowned)

30

When all the world shall be aloft,
Then Hallamshire shall be God's Croft.

(God's Croft was the name of a farmhouse lying halfway between Frogsham and Helsby, and supposed to be the place indicated by the prophet Nixon, when he was asked where a man should find safety on the Day of Judgement.)

*   *   *

O Skipton in Craven,
Is never a haven,
But many a day foul weather.

*   *   *

The low square tower of Hornsea once bore a tall spire, which fell in a gale in the year 1773, and there was a local superstition that a stone was found on the occasion with the following inscription:

Hornsea broth I built thee,
Thou was ten miles from Beverley,
Ten miles from Bridlington,
And ten miles from the sea.

*   *   *

The hospitality of the religious houses of East Yorkshire is referred to in the following rhyme:

If you go to Nun Keling, you shall find your body filling
Of whig or of whay,
But go to Swine, and come betime,
Or else you go empty away,
But the Abbot of Meaus does keep a good house,
By night and by day.

*   *   *

An old Yorkshire rhyme, said to have originated at the time of the suppression of the monasteries, runs thus:

I'll no more be a nun, nun, nun,
I'll no more be a nun, nun, nun,
But I'll be a wife and lead a merry life,
And brew good ale by the tun, tun, tun.

Paull, near Hull, one of many Yorkshire villages which forms the subject of a folk rhyme.

Whoso is hungry and lists well to eat,
Let him come to Sprotborough for his meat :
And for a night and for a day
His horse shall have both corn and hay,
And no man shall ask him when he goes his way.

(Sprotborough is 3½ miles south-west of Doncaster.)

*　　*　　*

Sutton, boiled mutton,
Brotherton beef,
Ferrybridge bonny lass,
And Knottingley thief.

*　　*　　*

High Paull, and Low Paull, and Old Paull town,
There is ne'er a maid married in all Paul town.

(These three villages are on the Yorkshire bank of the Humber. The explanation of this verse is that the church was half a mile distant from the three villages.)

Nothing at Tadcaster deserves a name,
But the fair bridge that's built without a stream.

(It is said that the water was so narrow that a bridge seemed hardly necessary.)

*   *   *

According to this old rhyme, the Lady Mayoress of York always retains her title:

He is a lord for a year and a day,
But she is Lady for ever and aye.

MANY old Yorkshire weather predictions were in rhyme, and Whitby had one that foretold fine weather was coming: "A Northern harr brings fine weather from far." (Hag or harr is mist with fine rain.) The following two verses also come from the Whitby area:

An old moon in a mist
Is worth gold in a kist,
But a new moon's mist
Will never lack thrist. (thirst)

* * *

When the sun sets black
A Westerly wind will not lack.

or

A sunset and a cloud so black,
A Westerly wind you shall not lack.

The following are used throughout Yorkshire:

When the mist comes from the hill
Then good weather it doth spill;
When the mist comes from the sea,
Then good weather it will be.

* * *

The wind at North and East
Is neither good for man nor beast,
So never think to cast a clout
Until the end of May is out.

* * *

A Southerly wind with showers of rain
Will bring the wind from West again.

* * *

*   *   *

Leeds has its own peculiar greeting to the snow:

("Bull" is possibly a corruption of "burl" to pour.)

Another verse about snow was recited by school-children:

And when the snow is abating:

When the children of the Whitby area saw the moon shining into their bedrooms, they used to say:

The couplet used by the children of Leeds varied slightly:

Other weather rhymes are:

*   *   *

Today, we switch on the television and watch a man predict the coming weather by means of complicated maps and charts, but are these new scientific methods any more reliable than those used in the olden days by the villagers? When you know how, the countryman's methods are very simple. He just studies nature and observes the actions of the birds, beasts, insects and plants, who by some uncanny means seem to know when the weather is likely to change.

By watching the birds, it is a simple matter to learn a great deal about the weather. If they suddenly become silent and there is a marked hush, you can be certain that it won't be long before you see a flash of lightning and hear a clash of thunder. When rooks and crows croak noisily and fly around their nests for no apparent reason, sailing about on motionless wings like kites, it is an omen that bad weather is on its way. When robins come near the door searching for food, it is a sure sign that there will be a snow storm. Even the wise old owl seems to hoot louder and more than usual when the weather is about to change, as if warning the other birds to shelter from the coming rain.

One of the smallest of nature's weather prophets is the spider. When fine weather is approaching, he will extend his web in all directions, and the threads that anchor it are always very long. When rain or storms are on their way, he spends his time strengthening his home and making the anchoring threads short so that they will stand up to the boisterous wind and wet. If you see a spider beginning to alter or rebuild his web in the evening, you can predict a fine and clear night, and if he carries out the same routine in the morning, you can be sure that it is going to be a fine and sunny day. When he breaks up his web and takes shelter in crevices, or under leaves, it is time to forecast bad weather.

Swarms of gnats, flying about in the evening sunshine, show that the next day is going to be warm and sunny, and if you see a large number of them in the spring the latter part of the year will be mild. Large numbers of bats and nocturnal beetles flying about foretell that the following day will be fine, but if the bees are reluctant to leave their hives it is a sure sign of rain.

When a countryman looks into a pond or pool to foretell the coming weather, he is not using it as a crystal but is observing the actions of the fish. If they swim near the surface of the water, and readily come up for food, it won't be long before the rain falls, but if they lurk at the bottom it will be some time before he sees rain. When toads and frogs are conspicuous, and croak loud and long, it is not advisable to go out without a raincoat or umbrella.

When your pet cat rubs its paws behind its ears, and the dog rolls on the floor, scratching itself, it is a sign of rain. If you see

Some creatures which predict the coming weather.

freshly thrown up mole hills, the weather is going to be wet and cold. This can be verified by observing the sheep and cattle, as they will huddle together in a corner or on the lee side of a tree or hedge. The sheep will chase each other round the field and turn their backs to the wind. Both horses and sheep stretch their necks in the air and sniff, as if they can smell the coming rain.

By observing the plants, one can tell what kind of weather to expect. When trees rustle their leaves in calm and still weather, they are waiting for the life-giving moisture, and it will not be long before large drops of rain herald the approaching storm. Even the blind are able to tell when the rain is on its way, because the scent of flowers is always much stronger. To the uninitiated all this may seem like magic, but to those who know nature's secrets it is just a matter of careful observation.

6. Yorkshire Superstitions

THE old people of Hull used to believe that if a man and wife washed in the same water they would be having a row before they went to bed. This is but one of many Yorkshire superstitions, some others being:

If your palm itches, you will be sure to get some money, either given or paid to you. Odd numbers are luckier than even numbers, and most deaths take place at the turn of the tide.

* * *

Children who cannot retain their water can be cured by eating three roasted mice. The same tasty dish is also a cure for whooping-cough.

* * *

If your right ear burns, some person is speaking well of you; but if your left ear burns then they are slandering you.

* * *

To discover the body of a drowned person, make a hole in the centre of a penny roll and fill it with quicksilver. Float this upon the water, and it will stand still over the place where the body lies.

* * *

When you hear a cuckoo, turn a penny over in your pocket and you will never be without one until you hear him again.

* * *

It is unlucky to kill a cricket. If you kill a beetle it is sure to rain. If you kill a small black spider, known as a "money spider", you will lose money somehow.

* * *

Be sure when you go to get married that you don't go in one door and out at another, or you will be very unlucky. Whoever goes to sleep first on the marriage night will be the first to die.

Happy is the bride that the sun shines on, and blessed is the corpse that the rain falls on.

* * *

It is unlucky to meet a funeral; to rob either a robin's or a swallow's nest; to cross your knife and fork, or spill the salt cellar; and to be first wished a Merry Christmas or a Happy New Year by a fair man.

* * *

You will marry the first man or woman, as the case may be, that you meet on Valentine morn. To dream of your sweetheart: Take the bladebone of a rabbit and stick nine pins into it, and then put it under your pillow. You will see the object of your affections in your dreams.

* * *

To cut a child's nails before it is twelve months old is very unlucky. If you wish well to your neighbour's child, when it first comes to your house, you must give it a cake, a little salt and an egg.

* * *

It is considered very lucky to find old iron, such as a rusty nail or a horseshoe. It is extremely lucky if the shoe has seven nails in it.

* * *

The country people of Yorkshire used to believe that night-flying white moths, especially the Hepialus Humuli, were souls of dead people, and it was unlucky to meet them on your nocturnal journeys.

* * *

Some Yorkshire folk will not burn elder wood because they believe Our Lord's cross was made of it. This is a Christianised version of the pagan belief that the elder was the sacred tree of the Mother Goddess, and it was an insult to her to burn the wood of her tree.

* * *

If the sun shines through the apple trees on Christmas Day, there will be an abundant crop the following year.

* * *

A person going to be married, on meeting a male acquaintance, always begins rubbing his elbow. When a newly married couple

Harvest time in Wharfedale in the pre-tractor age. A large number of superstitions are associated with harvesting.

first entered their house, a person brought in a hen and made it cackle to bring good luck to the newly married couple.

*   *   *

The Yorkshire children had their crow and lady-bird charms. When they saw a crow, which they considered an unlucky bird, they would say

> *Crow, crow, get out of my sight,*
> *Or else I'll eat thy liver and lights.*

They continued reciting this couplet until the bird flew away. If they found a lady-bird, they would place it on the palm of their hand and repeat the following incantation until it flew off:

Lady-bird, lady-bird, eigh thy way home;
Thy house is on fire, thy children all roam,
Except little Nan, who sits in her pan,
Weaving old lace as fast as she can.

(In Yorkshire, the lady-bird was also known as lady-cow, cow-lady and cusha-cow-lady.)

Yorkshire folk tried to predict from the number of magpies seen together. In the Whitby area, it was:

One is a sign of mischief,
Two is a sign of mirth,
Three is a sign of a wedding,
Four is a sign of death,
Five is a sign of rain,
Six is a sign of a bastard birth.

In the West Riding a farmer had lost many horses through sickness, and a person wished to buy one of the few left. The farmer refused, saying that if he buried the horse alive, the disease would end. This absurdity was fully believed.

In the East Riding the last load of the harvest was called the "Hockey". It was followed by men and boys singing and shouting the following:

We hev her, we hev her;
A coo in a tether;
At oor toon end;
A yow and a lamb,
A pot and a pan;
May we get seeaf in
Wiv oor harvest yam,
Wiv a sup o' good yal,
And sum haupence ti spend.
                    Hurrah!

When they returned to the stackyard, there was always scrambling for apples.

Another version of the harvest song was:

Here we cum at oor toonend,
A pint o' yal and a croon to spend.
Here we cum as tight as nip,
An nwyer flang ower, but yance wi a grip.

In Cleveland, on forking the last sheaf in the harvest field, they shouted in chorus:

Well bun, and better shorn,
Is Master — 's corn.
We hev her, we hev her,
As fast as a feather,
Hip, hip, hurrah!

The harvesters made merry at the local inn, and drank the harvest toast:

Here's a health to the barleymow,
Here's a health to the man who very well can
Both harrow and plough and sow.
When it is well sown,
See it is well mown.
Both raked and gravell'd clean,
And a barn to lay it in,
Here's a health to the man who very well can,
Both thrash and fan it clean.

In some old Yorkshire cottages, until quite recently, a ponderous necklace of "Lucky Stones" (i.e. stones with holes through them) hung up behind the door to ward off the "Yevil eye". I have heard that a woman in Catterick, at the beginning of this century, believed that one of the locals could look with the "yevil eye", and caused her daughter to fall into a pining sickness because she had some grudge against her. The doctors could do nothing for the girl and she died.

One old Yorkshire woman described how one could obtain the power of the evil eye: "Ye gang out ov' a night — every night, while ye find nine toads — an' when ye've gitten t' nine toads, ye hang 'em up on a string, an' ye make a hole and buries t' toads i' t' hole — and as t' toads pine away, so t' person pines away 'at you've looked upon wiv a yevil eye, an' they pine and pine away while they die, without ony disease at all."

Another old Yorkshire woman, when asked if she ever said her prayers at night, repeated the following:

From witches and wizards and long-legged buzzards,
And creeping things that run in hedge-bottoms,
Good Lord, deliver us.

In one of the principal Yorkshire towns, up to a century ago, it was the custom of upper and middle-class people to take children suffering from whooping-cough to a neighbouring convent. Here the priest would let them drink some holy water out of a silver chalice, which the sufferers were forbidden to touch. This was regarded as a sure remedy by both Protestants and Catholics alike.

At Bradfield in the parish of Ecclesfield, it was the custom when a death occurred for a person to be appointed to call the neighbours to the funeral in these words: "You are invited to the funeral of . . . which is to take place at . . . on . . . and there will be dinner on table at . . . o'clock." The same person would go to the bees' hives and deliver the same message, as it was thought that if this compliment was omitted the bees would die.

The old Yorkshire folk considered it was unlucky to have warts, and had several strange methods of charming them away. One of these was: "Steal a piece of meat from a butcher's stall, or his basket, and after having well rubbed the parts affected with the stolen morsel, bury it under a gateway at four lanes end, or in case of emergency, in any secluded place. All this must be done secretly to escape detection; and as the portion of meat decays, the warts will disappear."

Irish immigrants to Yorkshire had great faith in the following charm. When a funeral was passing by, they would rub the warts and say three times: "May these warts and this corpse pass away and never return, in the name of the Father, Son and Holy Ghost."

Other charms for warts were:
Touch each wart with a separate green pea, each pea being wrapped in paper by itself and burned. The warts will vanish as the peas turn to ashes.

*   *   *

Cut a slip of elder tree, and make a notch in it for every wart. Touch each wart with the twig and think no more about it. Do not even look at the warts or the charm will fail. Bury the twig without telling anyone where it is, and in about a week the warts will have gone.

*   *   *

Rub the warts with a bean swad, and throw the pod away. They will be gone within less than a fortnight.

*   *   *

Go to an ash tree in April or May, and take a packet of fresh pins. Stick one pin into the bark and then into the wart until it hurts. Then stick the pin back into the tree. Do this with a fresh pin for every wart. They will be gone within six weeks. (I have seen one such tree which was thickly studded with old pins, each one indicating a cured wart).

7

Wedding Wisdom

MANY a Yorkshire mother has told her daughter, who is about to be married, the old saying: "Happy is the bride-to-be who wakes to the singing of birds on her wedding day." If this happens, she will never quarrel with her husband, and the couple will always be constant to each other.

Marriage is rich in folklore and customs that are not generally known by those on the verge of matrimony. Did you know that the word "Wed" is from the Anglo-Saxon meaning "Pledge", as the two lovers pledge to abide by certain rules that are intended to bring happiness to both parties?

In olden days in Yorkshire the bride made all the wedding trousseau herself, and the bridal gown was made by her friends. The girls used to sew strands of their own hair into the hems to ensure that they would have early marriages. White became the colour of the bride because it represented purity, candour and simplicity, but the veils used by the ancient Greek and Roman brides were yellow, and covered them completely during the wedding ceremony.

The wearing of orange blossom was introduced into England from France in 1820. The white blossom symbolised innocence, while the tree from which it comes denotes abundance and prosperity. The chaplet of flowers worn on the bride's head, and the bouquet she carried, meant fruitfulness. In the Middle Ages, brides carried ears of corn for the same reason.

If a spider crawls on the bridal gown, it is a lucky omen and foretells wealth and plenty. It was once the custom in Yorkshire for the bride to feed all the stray cats before going to church. If they were black, and rubbed themselves against her, it was exceedingly lucky. After her final glance in the mirror, the bride had to add something new to her attire, such as a pair of gloves or a brooch. If she failed to do this, she would have no luck at all. If she cried before the ceremony, it was a very bad omen. The most unlucky thing was to pass a funeral on the way to the church.

The name "Bride" comes from St. Bridget, who is a Christianised version of the ancient Mother Goddess of Fertility. The girl symbolised the goddess on her wedding day, and it was hoped that she, too, would soon become a mother.

Originally, bread and salt were offered to the married couple to ensure that they would never want, but this was replaced by the wedding cake with its icing. This was first introduced in the reign of Charles II. For a guest to refuse a piece of the cake showed that the person wished the bride ill fortune. If the toast was drunk in water, or a soft drink, it was sure to bring misfortune and trouble.

When removing the bridal dress and veil, the bride had to remove all the pins and either give them to her female friends or throw them away. If she threw them in the air, the girl who caught the most would be the next bride. If she used any of the pins in her going-away dress, bad luck would follow her and her honeymoon would not be a happy one. The honeymoon is so called because the Teutons used to celebrate a wedding by drinking mead, a drink made from honey, for thirty days after the event. The couple did not go off on their own, but stayed and joined in the merrymaking. Quarrels on the honeymoon were said to predict a happy and harmonious future.

In some parts of the North, the groom had to carry his bride over the threshold of the house, and often water was poured over the threshold before the bride crossed it. Sometimes, a cake of oats was broken over the wife's head to make sure the newly weds would never want.

One had to walk into the church with the right foot first, and to stumble was a bad omen. To make sure of their future happiness, the couple had to smile at each other when they met at the altar. That is why the groom kept his back turned as the bride walked down the aisle.

The groom had also to look out for pitfalls. Once he had started out for the church, he hadn't to go back. If he found he had left something at home, he had to send the best man back to get it. He had to be careful not to drop the ring, and had to push it as far down the bride's finger as possible. If he failed to do this, it was a sign that they would soon be parted. If she had to help him to do this, it was a sure sign that she would wear the trousers and rule the home.

June was, and still is, the most popular month for weddings. The name comes from Juno, the wife of Jupiter, who was believed by the Romans to be the protector of women. Some Christians used to refuse to get married on a Friday because it was the day of the Crucifixion, and according to others it was the day that Adam and Eve ate the forbidden fruit. Non-Christians believe it is the luckiest day of the week because it is dedicated to Venus, Goddess of Love and Beauty. Although there is no particular reason for it, Monday is not a popular day for weddings, but Wednesdays and Saturdays are. Personally, I cannot see what difference the day makes, but here is an old country rhyme that professes to know why wedding days should be carefully chosen:

Monday for Health,
Tuesday for Wealth,
Wednesday the best day of all,
Thursday for Losses,
Friday for Crosses,
Saturday has no luck at all.

8

Penny Gaffs

YORKSHIRE folk were always attracted by fairs, and both town and country people looked forward to the days when the showmen's waggons trundled into their neighbourhood. It was the time of merriment for both young and old.

Like the music halls and other British traditions, the fairs are slowly being strangled to death by television and town-planning. Those that still remain are pitiful sights compared with the fairs that used to tour our country during the summer months. A few rides, a shooting gallery, a Gipsy palmist and several "Bingo" stalls are all that remain — all the fun of the fair seems to have completely vanished. The side shows, with their fat women, tattooed ladies, snake-charmers and other oddities, are now a thing of the past. It has been said that P. T. Barnum, the American showman, was the first to exhibit freaks of nature, but such novelties were shown at fairs, inn yards and other suitable places back in medieval times.

Let us go back a century and see what the people of our county could witness for the modest fee of one penny. The majority of freaks that came to Britain were first exhibited in London, and when their popularity dwindled they toured the rest of the country before going over to the continent. These people worked on a fifty-fifty basis, receiving one half of the takings. They began work as soon as the first visitor arrived on the fairground and continued until late at night when the people started drifting away home.

Perhaps the most famous of all freaks to visit Yorkshire were the Siamese Twins, and more has been written about them in medical journals than any other misformed creature. Eng and Chang were born in Siam in 1811. Their father was Chinese and had gone to Siam where he married a daughter of another China-man. Their mother was thirty-five at the time of their birth, and had previously given birth to four female babies, and eventually had fourteen children in all. It was only with difficulty that their lives were spared, as Chowpahyi, the King of Siam, believed that the birth of such monsters would bring evil to the country and wanted them destroyed.

In 1824, a British merchant named Hunter saw the twins
stripped to the waist, and persuaded the king and their parents
to allow them to go on exhibition. They were taken from the
country by a Captain Coffin, and after an eight week tour in the
United States they arrived in London in 1829. After a long tour
in Britain, they were supposed to go to France, but the French
authorities would not allow them in the country because they
thought their appearance might affect pregnant women and cause
them to give birth to monsters.

They returned to America, and settled down as farmers in
North Carolina, under the name Bunker. When they were forty-
four years old, they married two English sisters, twenty-six and
twenty-eight years of age respectively. Owing to domestic diffi-
culties, they kept their wives in separate houses and lived with
each one on alternate weeks. It was rumoured that after many
quarrels the twins decided to revisit England to consult the most
famous surgeons on the advisability of being separated. This was
quite untrue, and was purely a method of gaining publicity, as

**A typical poster from the golden age
of shows and fairs.**

they were short of money and wanted to exhibit themselves again. Newspaper reports caused the English people to flock to see the famous twins before they became separate people. They died on January 17th, 1874.

About the year 1857 an advertisement appeared in the papers stating that "The Woolly Woman of Hayti" had arrived in England and would tour the country. Handbills were distributed throughout the towns and pictured a beautiful creature with long flowing silken hair. You can imagine how disappointed the people were when the curtain was pulled back and revealed a shrivelled old woman, as black as a crow, with hair as crisp and as woolly as the coat of a sheep. Her name was Antoinette, and she was obviously a negress from Africa. She was fifty-eight years old, and her hair did not begin to grow until ten years before she went on exhibition. She had a long, thick, plaited mass of wool-like hair that was allowed to hang down on her right side. It was four feet eight inches long, and grew from the top of her head. The total weight of the hair was said to be four pounds. According to Frank Buckland, M.A., who took a great interest in the freaks of his day, Antoinette suffered from a form of disease called plica polonica, which caused the hair to become matted together and in those days was not uncommon among the Jews of Poland. There are three examples of this type of hair in the College of Surgeons.

Antoinette did not make her fortune in Britain, and her downfall was due to a squabble with a giant named Brice. He was exhibited in a sort of Indian temple at the Cremorne Gardens, and for a long time had had this place all to himself. When the "Woolly Woman" returned to London it was decided that the temple should be divided in two, so that she could share it with the giant, but he flew into a temper and threatened to leave. As the giant was considered to be the best attraction, poor Antoinette had to depart. She went to Paris and that was the last that was heard of her.

Joseph Brice, the French giant, also visited Yorkshire. He was twenty-two years of age, stood eight feet high, and weighed thirty stones. At Sheffield he got into trouble for looking out of the windows of the house where he stayed. The man who had agreed to pay him for a certain number of exhibitions observed a crowd staring up at the house. He rushed upstairs and found Brice looking out of the windows that were a great height from the floor. The showman said the giant had broken his contract as he was letting the townsfolk see him for nothing. Brice said that the tallest men he had met came from Yorkshire, and recalled a John Greeve from Pontefract who was just under seven feet.

In 1865, when Peto, the giant of Fychow, was advertised, it

was stated, "His height is stupendous, his strength Herculean and his weight four tons." Poor old Brice got very worried — he thought he had a rival at last. However, his fears were groundless, as Peto was a four-legged giant. In fact, he was just a very fine elephant, and his showman thought this method of advertising was a capital idea to cause a sensation.

During that year a woman named Julia Pastrama toured the country. She was remarkable for the immense quantity of long black hair that grew on and about her face. It was stated that she was found among the tribes of Dregiy Indians who inhabited parts of Mexico. When she died in Moscow, she was not allowed to rest in peace, and her days of showbusiness were not over. She was embalmed by a Professor Suckaloff, and her mummy went on exhibition. There was nothing horrific or unpleasant about the mummy, and Julia appeared exactly as she had done when alive. She was taken on a tour of England as "The Embalmed Nondescript".

Not all freaks were what they were supposed to be, and "The Spotted Child", who was covered from head to foot with spots of all shapes and sizes and was exhibited in Yorkshire around 1862, was made into a freak of nature by her mother. The woman obtained the effect by painting spots on her six-year-old daughter with nitrate of silver. It did not harm the child and soon wore off.

The year 1867 saw "The Monster Pig". It stood 4ft 6ins high, was 12ft long, had a girth of 8ft 6ins and weighed 200 stones. It was still growing, and competent judges thought it would make 300 stones.

The mermaid craze was started by P. T. Barnum, and many were exhibited throughout England. Although they were depicted on the advertisements as the conventional, beautiful, half-woman half-fish, the actual exhibits were dried-up, black-looking creatures about three feet long. They were made by Japanese fishermen who managed to unite the upper half of a monkey to the lower half of a fish.

"Mermaids", made in Japan by grafting a monkey to a fish, were once a popular source of entertainment.

One of the last freaks to visit Yorkshire was the Great Omi,
who appeared at a fun-fair in Scarborough. He was a unique
tattooed man, his head, face and complete body being covered
with dark blue stripes and scrolls like a zebra. He was the
youngest son of a well-to-do family, and was educated at a well-

**The Great Omi, king of tattooists,
who had 15 million needle pricks in
order to complete his facial designs.**

known public school. He took up an army career and rose to the
rank of major. Fairgrounds and circuses had always fascinated
him, and when he left the army he tried to get a job as a bare-
back rider, but found there were better men at it than himself.
He finally decided to become a tattooed man, but he had to be
different from all the rest. In 1927 he put himself in the hands
of George Burchett, a London tattooist, and went through as
many as five hundred operations before the designs on his body
were completed. It took more than 150 hours, spread over a
year, and 15,000,000 needle pricks to complete the facial designs,
and as many as 500,000,000 to cover his torso. It cost about
£1,000.

To become a freak in order to earn a living is a gamble, but in
the case of the Great Omi it came off. After starting with
Bertram Mills at the London Olympia, he went to America and
appeared with Ripley's "Believe It or Not" show, the Ringling
Brothers' Circus and at Madison Square Gardens. He commanded
some of the biggest fees in showbusiness. During the war he
returned to England and took part in charity shows all over the
country. When peace returned, he again toured the North. He
always kept his real name a secret, but one Yorkshireman who
had served in the first world war recognised the Great Omi as

his old Commanding Officer. However, he promised to keep the secret. George Burchett, the tattooist, also knew the identity of the Great Omi, but took the secret with him to the grave.

It was the Whitby hero, Captain Cook, who brought the first tattooed man to England. He was a native of Amsterdam in the South Seas whose name was Omai. He was exhibited all over Britain by Cook's companion, Sir Joseph Banks, and when Cook left England in 1776 on another voyage of discovery he took Omai on board the *Resolution* and returned him to his native land.

The most famous tattoo artist of the late Victorian and Edwardian era was a Yorkshireman. He was Tom Riley, dapper and talkative, but also a shrewd businessman and a wonderful tattooist. He was said to have the talents of a great painter and the bearings of a Harley Street surgeon. Tom Riley was born in Leeds and began his craft when he was in the army. After his service in the forces, he returned to Leeds and took drawing lessons at the Mechanics' Institute. After opening his first work-room in Liverpool's dockyard, he moved to Glasgow. His fame spread rapidly, and he was invited to become the resident tattooist at the Royal Aquarium in London. Later, he started his own surgery in the Strand, and built up a clientele of society people. Among his customers were Nicholas II, Czar of Russia; King Oscar of Sweden; Kaiser Wilhelm II; the Khedive Abbas of Egypt; and last but not least, King Edward VII, when he was still Prince of Wales. Among his first ladies of distinction to acquire a dainty tattoo was Lady Randolph Churchill, the American born mother of Sir Winston Churchill.

That period was the golden age of spectacular tattooing, and the business flourished on both sides of the Atlantic. It was while in America that Tom Riley was given the title of "Professor" by that Prince of Showmen and self-styled "King of Humbug", Phineas Taylor Barnum. From that day, all other tattooists took the title "Professor".

From early times until the second world war many travelling "mountebanks" visited the English town and villages, and Yorkshire had its fair share of these performers. They would do their acts in any odd space that was available, and earned a scanty living from the coppers they could collect from the spectators. Some of those who turned up in Yorkshire at the start of this century are worth mentioning.

One man, with an enormous stock of wool-like hair, would hold his nose with his fingers and produce the sounds of a donkey braying. Another used to carry a wash tub about with him, and whenever he found water available he would fill the tub and gather a crowd around him. Then he would throw a small coin into the tub, as a decoy for other contributions, and

A Punch and Judy show in Leeds Road, Sheffield, at the turn of the century.

by putting his head under the water would fish out the coins with his lips. For many years, a grim and dirty looking old man pushed a model of a coal mine hundreds of miles around the Yorkshire towns and villages on an old pram. A placard on his hat stated that he had been blown up by fire-damp, which prevented him from future work. Another wanderer, with an electric machine, used to offer shocks at the rate of a penny a shock, or three for twopence. The shocks were believed to be good for the health.

The "Living Salamander" was a regular visitor. He would take some dirty tow and powdered resin from his pocket, place it on an old tin plate and set it alight. He would then cut up the smoking and indigestible meal with a knife and fork and eat it all up. Having done this, he then devoured a hatful of paper shavings, and proceeded to draw from his mouth yards and yards of multi-coloured paper ribbon.

The "Infant Hercules" was the title assumed by a six-foot man with limbs like a giant. His pale, half-starved looking wife would hand him a cup and a heavy metal ball. He tied the cup to his forehead and then, throwing the ball into the air, would catch it in the cup. He staggered as the heavy ball entered the cup with a thud. Then, taking two cannon balls from a sack, he tossed them about as though they were made of cork. He made them run up one arm, across his back, down the other arm and back again. By simply straightening his elbow joint, he caused them to jump up and down in the air, and do everything that seemed contrary to the law of gravity. The cannon balls were genuine articles, and were handed out for examination while his wife collected contributions in an old hat.

The "India-rubber Man" turned his body into sundry positions, and then did a very foolish and dangerous trick with a needle. He placed it point uppermost in the ground and drew it out by causing the needle point to just enter the skin of his eyelids. All the time he was doing this his body was bent in an abnormal position, somewhat like a Z.

Numerous Punch and Judy men used to push their little stages around the county and set up in some side street. They used to be known as "Kerb Street Professors". The shrill squeak of Mr. Punch soon caused a crowd to gather round the red and white striped booth. Motor cars and traffic control have driven these puppeteers from our streets, and national assistance, although a good thing, has robbed us of many different alfresco entertainments.

9. Things that go Bump in the Night

IN parts of Yorkshire, when a person was buried the mourners used to throw rosemary or some other herb into the grave. This was done to make the spirit rest. During the absence of the funeral party, the position of the furniture in the sickroom of the deceased was changed, with the intention of deceiving the ghost so that it would not recognise its home if it returned and would leave the family in peace. These precautions could not have been very successful, judging by the number of ghosts that are supposed to haunt Yorkshire.

One legend avers that Guy Fawkes still haunts his old home at Scotton. Just before midnight the spectre approaches the main door, stops, shakes its head and then vanishes. It is also said to appear between six and seven o'clock every Bonfire Night.

Mary Queen of Scots is believed to haunt Nappa Hall, where she once spent two nights as the guest of Sir Christopher Metcalf. Some of the old inhabitants of Sheffield said they had seen the Queen's ghost at Manor Lodge where she was once imprisoned. Walton Abbey, near Driffield, has a ghost of a lady who was murdered by the Roundheads during the Civil War. Her headless ghost, carrying a child, has haunted the Abbey ever since.

Some years ago the people who lived in the Abbey House of Kirkstall in Leeds were troubled with a ghost. A monk is also said to haunt the Rectory of Bolton. In 1911 the Rev. James McNabb was standing by the window of an empty room, and when he turned round he saw the ghost standing in the doorway. After a few seconds it vanished. It was believed to be the ghost of a monk who was murdered for the sake of relics he was carrying from one community to another. In 1931 a ghost of a tall monk was seen at St. Michael's Church, Linton. It only appeared on Fridays, and was influenced by music. One afternoon the rector was sitting playing the organ when he heard footsteps behind him. He turned and saw a very tall figure; it was wearing a heavy cowl but he could see no face.

Leeds ghosts do not always choose buildings for their nightly visitations. The White Lady of Richmond Hill haunted the top of the rise of that name. People who lived in the district in the

1850s believed the ghost was that of a devout young woman who died in tragic circumstances on her twentieth birthday.

Heath Old Hall, near Wakefield, was haunted by the spirit of Mary Bolles, who died there in 1662, leaving elaborate instructions concerning her funeral. This was to cost no less than £1,220, of which £700 was for mourning garments, £400 for incidental expenses and £120 for entertaining all visitors for the six weeks her corpse should be left before burial. It was not long before her spectre appeared, as she was troubled about some unfulfilled detail of her will. The ghost was finally layed in a cavity which became known as Bolles Pit.

Whitby and Beverley have stories of coaches driven by skeletons. Flamborough has its White Lady at Dane's Dyke and its Headless Lady at Tramner Hall. Scarborough boasts of several ghosts. There is a lady with a loaf of bread on her head who haunts the *Three Mariners Inn;* there is a headless woman who walks Quay Street; and a phantom coach, drawn by five horses, which drives day and night. The fishing village of Staithes is not without a ghostly visitor. It seems that some centuries ago two sisters named Grundy suddenly fell over the cliff; one of them cut her head off on the sharp rocks and her ghost still haunts the shore.

**Kirkstall Abbey, near Leeds. People
in the Abbey House have often been
troubled with a ghost.**

Ghosts are not a thing of the past, and many modern people claim they have seen them. A few years ago the newspapers came out with the story about Yorkshire's haunted golf course at Howley Hall, situated on a hill between Morley and Batley. According to some of the locals, it is not just a single ghost but a number of spectres which move about the greens and fairways and then vanish.

Mr. Gordon Bunney, of Leeds, told the reporters that he and his wife were strolling along the edge of the links, near the ruins of the old hall, when she remarked about the strange costume of a woman walking towards them. She wore a long dress with a red veil over her face and shoulders. Suddenly, she slowly vanished before their eyes. Tom Comersall, a mill-worker of Batley Carr, saw two men and a woman whom he thought were golfers. When his dog started to bark and began running towards them they also disappeared. Some of the club members were sceptical, but a director of a Dewsbury mill said he was playing golf on his own, when it was getting dusk, and he felt he was

**The ghost of St. Michael's church,
Linton, only walks on Fridays.**

being watched by a whole crowd of people. He looked around, but there was nobody in the vicinity. He admitted it was a most unpleasant experience and he couldn't get back to the club house quick enough.

The builder of the old hall was John Savile, the first Mayor of Leeds, who died in 1603 and was buried in Batley parish church. His son inherited the estate, and during the Civil War he joined the King, leaving the Hall in charge of a relation, Sir John Savile of Lupset, near Wakefield. When the royalist Duke of Newcastle approached the Hall with his army, he demanded that it should be handed over in the King's name, but Sir John was stubborn and refused to do it. A siege ensued, and with a handful of servants Sir John managed to hold off the forces for a few days. Newcastle brought up some cannon and blasted the Hall to ruins, looted the valuables and killed most of the defenders. William Smith, a gamekeeper, who finally opened the door to the Duke, was hacked to pieces. Sir John was imprisoned in Pontefract Castle. Could it be the shades of Sir John's retainers who appear and vanish on the golf course?

Some people thought that the ghosts were connected with the *Heedless Arms* which is situated a few hundred yards from the course, as it was the scene of a violent murder in 1670. The innkeeper, a Scot named Fletcher, recognised one of his customers as a highwayman called William Nevison. The landlord slipped out of the inn, and after locking his visitor's horse in the stable went to get help to catch the criminal. Nevison, realising what was happening, chased the innkeeper over the moors and stabbed him to death with a cobbler's knife. After the murder, the knight of the road freed his mare, Brown Bess, and rode to York. There he appeared on the bowling green, hoping to establish an alibi for himself. He was finally arrested near Wakefield and hanged at York Castle. Nevison's exploit has been attached to Dick Turpin and his famous ride to York.

One of the most unusual hauntings happened at Barnsley in recent years, and began when a fourteen-year-old boy was lying ill in bed. Michael Collindridge was staying at the *Cranberry Hotel* in Dodsworth Road which belonged to his grandmother. On the day that the manifestation started, Mrs. Collindridge had moved an old walking stick from the corner of the boy's bedroom and hung it over the bed-head. Suddenly, Michael shouted down to her that the stick was dancing and preventing him from going to sleep. She removed the stick and hung it on the banister at the top of the stairs. Within minutes Michael called her again to say the stick was still rattling. When she went up to him, the stick jumped from the banister and hung itself on the bedroom door. She put it on top of the wardrobe, but it jumped down on to a chair and then carried on doing various antics.

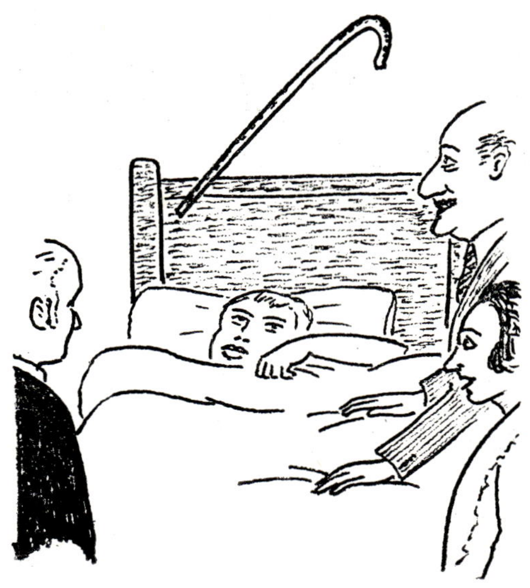

**The jumping stick at Barnsley, one
of the most recent of Yorkshire
poltergeist phenomena.**

Many locals saw the jumping stick, and two doctors examined
the boy, while Mr. Gordon Jepson, a Barnsley town councillor,
searched the room for hidden threads, but none was found. He
had to admit that it was the most fascinating thing that he had
ever seen. The story of the dancing stick spread through Yorkshire, and the national press moved in. A reporter of *The People*
wrote: "There was no metal connection through which the stick
could be manipulated. I examined it carefully. It was a very light
stick and worn with years of use. There is nothing to indicate
what made it perform. I don't believe it, but I saw it happen."
Mr. Ron Lane of the *Sheffield Morning Telegraph* took pictures
while the stick was dancing.

When it was discovered that young Michael had dabbled in
conjuring, and had performed at several children's parties, people
began to believe it was all a trick. David Nixon, the television
magician, when asked his opinion, said: "If this is a trick, then
Michael is a very remarkable boy. I would have to see the stick
in action before I could say if it was a trick. There are various
ways it might be done, but I gather that this is a perfectly

ordinary walking stick, not a conjurer's prop. I have done
levitation tricks, but I don't know whether I could fool twenty
reporters at close quarters as Michael has done."

I have spoken to several people who witnessed the dancing
stick. Some belonged to psychical research societies, and they
all swore it was perfectly genuine. If this is so, then Yorkshire
has the most perfect example of poltergeist phenomena that has
ever been recorded.

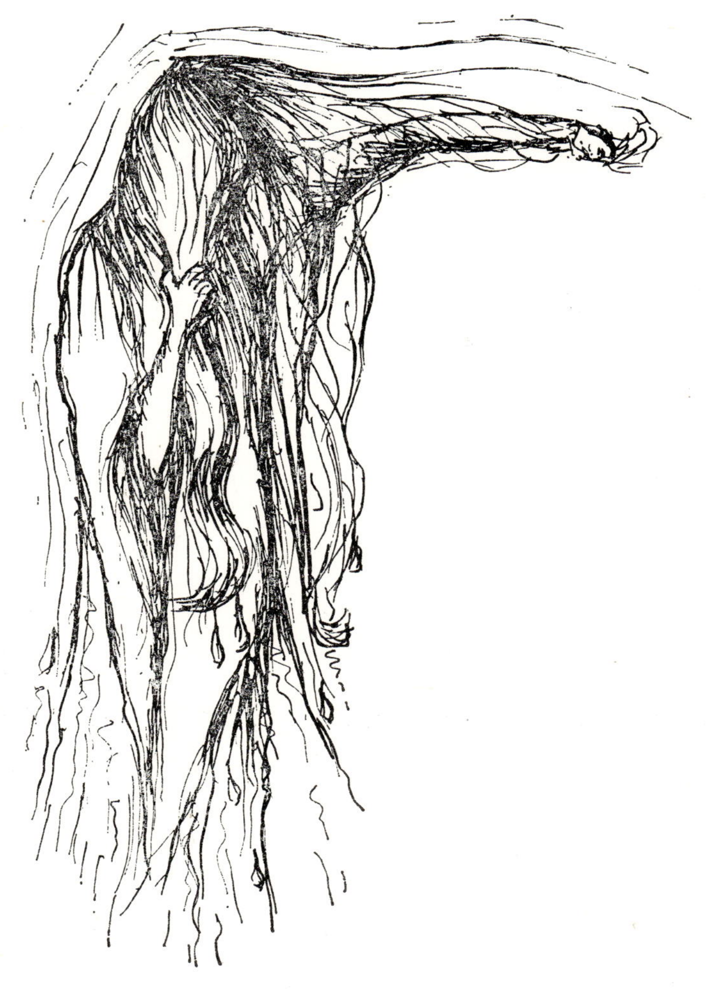

IN 1770 an eccentric weaver by the name of Thomas Hill began to construct a dwelling place out of the solid rock at Knaresborough. It took sixteen years to complete, and consisted of a number of rooms, one above the other, and had a fine view over the river Nidd. He called the place Fort Montague in honour of the Duchess of Buccleuch who once visited him. The locals dubbed him with the title of Sir Thomas Hill, but the weaver cared little about what the people thought of him. Later, he gave himself the title of Governor of Fort Montague, and issued notes valued at two and a half pence which resembled the old five pound notes.

Swinsty Hall, a remote farmhouse in the Washburn Valley, is said to have been built by a poor man who lived in London during the time of the plague. He stole a bag of gold from an untenanted house, whose owner had died of the disease, and fled to a deserted part of the country where he built the farmstead with the stolen money.

The inhabitants of Harpham, in East Yorkshire, began to hear drumming noises coming from an old well. The sound was said to have been made by a little drummer boy whose body was thrown into the well by an old man who murdered him. Whenever the drumming is heard, a death is supposed to occur in the village. Another story tells us that the little boy was playing and got lost in a tunnel that led to the well.

The tallest monolith in Britain can be seen standing among the graves in the churchyard of Rudston, near Driffield. Although the church is Norman, the stone dates back to between 1600 and 1000 B.C. It is $25\frac{1}{2}$ feet high, and weighs some forty tons, and is believed to be of the same dimensions underground. It is all that remains of a sacred site which belonged to the pre-Christian religion of these islands, and may be the last of many stones that once formed a circle. The rest would be broken up and used to build part of the church, and it is thought that this one was too much trouble to uproot. It remains one of the wonders of prehistoric Britain, and shows that our ancestors were not the ignorant savages that some historians would have us believe. Like other such stones in Yorkshire it has a legend connected with the Devil. In this case Satan was said to have aimed it at the church to destroy it, but missed. There are similar stories in Britain, which seems to prove that His Satanic Majesty must have been a very poor shot.

Richmond parish church is the only one in the country to have a number of shops built into it. It all happened because the church authorities became short of funds, so they let the lower part of the building as shops and offices and kept the rest of the church for services.

Pannal churchyard has a somewhat gruesome relic from the days of the body snatchers, when "resurrection men" dug up newly buried corpses to sell to medical men for dissecting purposes. There is a slab of stone that weighs over a ton, and requires over ten men to move it. This was hired by bereaved families to be placed over new graves to protect the corpse from being dug up. As the body snatchers usually worked in pairs, they would be unable to shift the stone. When this occupation became extinct the stone slab was converted into a shallow trough by a local farmer, but a few years ago it was rescued and returned to the churchyard where it still remains.

Visitors to Haworth churchyard are attracted to one of the

Swinsty Hall, said to have been built with stolen money. The finials above the doorway were to prevent the entry of witches.

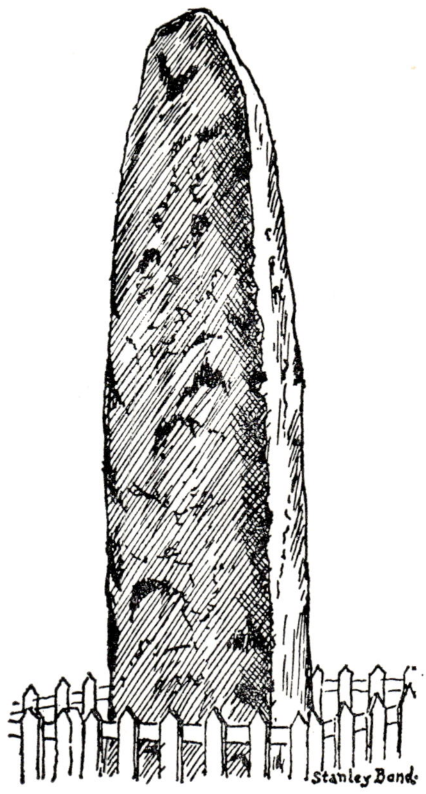

The monolith at Rudston, near Driffield, is the tallest in Britain.

tombstones which has a balloon carved upon it. The story goes that a Captain Bidmead of London flew over the district in a balloon. He was accompanied by a Miss Lilly Cove, who intended to make a parachute jump from the basket that hung from the balloon. An excited crowd gathered to watch her thrilling descent, but the parachute failed to open. Miss Cove fell in a field near Ponden and was killed. Her remains are buried under this distinctive tombstone. This is not the only unusual tombstone in Yorkshire. Kildwick churchyard has one in the form of an organ, and Otley has one in the shape of a railway tunnel. This was constructed as a memorial to some navvies who were accidentally killed when the nearby Bramhope Tunnel was being excavated.

A stone pyramid stands over the grave of Charles Piazzi Smith in Sharow churchyard. He was the Astronomer Royal for Scotland, but was chiefly known for his studies of the Great Pyramid of Gizeh. He believed that the various measurements of the pyramid corresponded with various events in the Bible. This suggestion was ridiculed by many learned people.

Close to the *Dick Hudson Inn,* near Bingley, a stone marks the spot where a poacher shot a gamekeeper in 1861, and a small stone cross beside the Malton-Scarborough road is said

to mark the grave of a gipsy's child. A black monument near Wold Newton shows us where a large meteorite fell on 13th December, 1795. The meteorite itself is in the London Museum. Close beside the road leading from Aberford to the village of Saxton, there stands a column that marks the site of one of the bloodiest battles fought in England — the Battle of Towton. In 1461, on Palm Sunday, sixty thousand supporters of the House of Lancaster fought fifty thousand Yorkists, and decided the War of the Roses. The Yorkists were victorious, and put Edward IV on the throne. The battle lasted all day and thirty thousand men lost their lives. Another souvenir of the War of the Roses is the chantry on Wakefield Bridge. It was built by King Edward IV in memory of his father who was killed by Lancastrians at the Battle of Wakefield in 1460.

Whitby Abbey, established in 657 A.D. by St. Hilda, has many legends connected with its founder.

Although the most well-known Yorkshire song is "On Ilkley Moor Baht 'At", there is no such place officially known as Ilkley Moor. The area overlooking Ilkley is marked on ordnance survey maps as Rombald's Moor. The tune of this song was often used for the hymn "While Shepherds Watched Their Flocks by Night". It is believed that the comedy words were written to enable choirboys to learn the tune more easily — this was quite a common custom in olden days.

Most of Yorkshire's abbeys and monasteries were built in valleys among the trees, and often a babbling brook passed close by. Whitby Abbey is an exception to this rule, and stands high up on the headland of the old town. It is the focal point for miles around, especially in these days as the ruins are floodlit. The original abbey was founded as a centre of learning by St. Hilda in 657 A.D., but was destroyed by the Danes 210 years later. A new one was built by the Benedictines in 1087, and the present ruins date back to the thirteenth century. They were bombed by the Germans during the last war.

There are many legends about St. Hilda, but the most interesting one tells how, like St. Patrick, she was associated with snakes.

We are told that the area around the abbey was infested by poisonous snakes, so St. Hilda prayed that they might be driven into the sea. Then she took a whip and drove hundreds of snakes over the cliff, first cutting off their heads with a single stroke. As each snake fell it coiled itself up and turned into stone. For centuries the locals believed this legend, and pointed out the number of stones found on the seashore that resembled coiled-up snakes. These were ammonites which are quite common in the Whitby area and are really fossilised sea-creatures — the crest of Whitby represents three of these fossils. It is also said that the seagulls dip their wings when flying over the abbey in honour of St. Hilda. There is a St. Hilda's Well at Hinderwell, and we are told that it was a stopping-place for the monks as they walked from Kirkham Abbey to Whitby.

In the early days of 1960 the vicar of Newby church, near Ripon, took a photograph of the altar. When the film was developed it revealed a hooded ghost, about nine feet high, standing by the altar. The negative was carefully examined and checked, but no evidence of a fault or fake could be found. The church was built in 1870, and there have never been any ghost stories connected with it.

St. Hilda's Well at Hinderwell was reputedly a stopping - place for monks.

To bring this chapter right up to date, it is necessary to mention that Yorkshire also has connections with flying saucers. On 28th March, 1966, Stephen Pratt and his mother were returning home in the evening from a fish and chip shop in Conisborough when they saw a bright orange light in the sky. The light seemed to throb and hover, as it approached the west. Stephen ran and fetched his camera and took a photograph, and three objects that resemble flying saucers were recorded on the negative. The boy's father also saw the light. The young man was ridiculed by his workmates who refused to believe his story, but when interviewed on television both he and his mother stuck to their account. Anyone who has seen the photograph would swear it was a picture of UFOs.

Two years later on 4th March, 1968, Alec Birch, a fourteen-year-old boy of Mosborough, Sheffield, took a photograph of flying saucers from his back garden. He told the newspaper reporter: "I suddenly saw five objects in the sky about 500 feet up. They were not moving and made no sound. Although the possibility that they might have been flying saucers did not cross my mind at the time, I took a photograph of them." His two friends also saw the strange objects. The objects in the picture certainly resemble our idea of flying saucers, but when the photograph was sent to the Air Ministry no satisfactory explanation was given.

Surviving Customs

THE world's oldest horse race is held every year at South Dalton on the third Thursday of March. It is called the Kiplingcotes Derby, and the course is said to be the first race-course to be laid out in Britain. It was first held in 1519 and was run at intervals for nearly a hundred years. In 1618 Lord Burlington and another Yorkshire squire invested a sum of money to make sure that the race would be held annually. It starts at 11 a.m. and goes through several parishes. It is the only race in which the winner receives less money than the runner-up, as the winner receives the interest on the investment, which is about five pounds, and the holder of the second place gets the stake money, which can be over twenty pounds.

The ringing of the Pancake Bell still takes place in Scarborough. About a century ago the bell hung in St. Thomas's Hospital, and was used as a curfew bell at 6 a.m. and 6 p.m. daily. On Shrove Tuesday it was rung at noon as a signal to housewives to start making the traditional pancakes. When the hospital was demolished the bell was removed to the museum, and it is still rung every Shrove Tuesday to keep up the old tradition. Many people ask, "Why do we have pancakes on this day?" The reason goes back to the pre-Reformation days, when all eggs and butter in the house had to be used up before Ash Wednesday as they could not be eaten during Lent. It was also the last day before Easter for merrymaking, so a general holiday was proclaimed when sports of every kind including pancake racing took place.

Scarborough also keeps up Shrovetide Skipping. Long skipping ropes are taken to the seashore, and fishermen and townsfolk continue skipping until dusk. Skipping was used as an old fertility rite to obtain good crops, and in fishing villages it was done to make sure of a good catch.

The ancient city of York has retained many old customs. At the York Assizes the Lady Mayoress presents the judge with a silver casket that contains sweet-smelling herbs. It is a survival of a much earlier custom of presenting a bouquet to ward off jail fever. Sometimes the City Sheriff gives the judge a pair of white gloves to show there are no prisoners for trial. Each year, on Lord Mayor's Day, the retiring Mayor gives the new Sheriff's Lady the Lady Mayoress's staff of honour, with instructions that she is to use it "to keep the Sheriff in order". She retains it until the reception at the Mansion House, which takes place two or three weeks later. At eight o'clock each evening a bell is rung in the church of St. Michael, Spurriergate. It is believed that the sound of the bell helped to guide travellers through the nearby Forest of Galtres. A large lamp used to hang in the tower of All Saints' Pavement for the same purpose; the tower is still illuminated at night to commemorate this old beacon light.

At Whitby, on the morning of Ascension Eve, a hedge of sticks and branches is built near the water's edge. It is called the Penny Hedge, and must be strong enough to withstand three tides. The first was built in 1160. It is said that a hermit monk gave refuge to a hunted boar, and that the hunters beat the hermit with their staves. Before he died the hermit asked the Abbot of Whitby to spare their lives. He agreed on the condition that the men did penance by building a hedge on the sands each year. This penance became a traditional custom, and "Penance Hedge" became corrupted into "Penny Hedge".

At nine o'clock every night in Ripon the Mayor's hornblower keeps up the custom of sounding the curfew. It is believed to date from the time of Alfred the Great. Dressed in a fawn coat, and wearing a three-cornered hat and gloves, he stands in the Market Place and blows a huge buffalo horn, which is nearly one hundred years old. A much older horn, dating from 1690,

The procession at Ripon's Feast of
St. Wilfrid in 1844.

69

hangs in the Mayor's Parlour; it is used on special occasions.

Wilfrid was an English saint who lived in Saxon times, and about A.D. 665 was made Bishop of York. He had some disagreement with the Archbishop of Canterbury and left the country. The Feast of St. Winfrid is held on the first Saturday in August, and commemorates his return from exile. In Ripon he is impersonated by a townsman who rides round the streets on a white horse, led by a monk and followed by a band. He makes his way to the cathedral, where the Dean is waiting to welcome him. On this day there is usually a fair in Ripon market square.

During the summer months a huge buffalo horn hangs in the entrance of the *Rose and Crown* inn at Bainbridge. From September to the following spring it is sounded nightly at 10 p.m. This custom has gone on for 700 years, to guide travellers who got lost on the moors or in the forests that surround the village.

Richmond, which was chosen as the typical English town in 1945, has an old custom that takes place in the cobbled market place on a convenient Saturday in September. The Mayor presents a bottle of wine to the first local farmer to bring a sample of new wheat to the market cross. The winning farmer must offer drinks all round and toast the health of the Mayor. He is then given a second bottle so he can celebrate with his family at home.

For more than 700 years the people of Dewsbury have listened to what is known as "Tolling the Devil's Knell". The church bell is tolled for a long period on Christmas Eve to celebrate the fact that the birth of Jesus heralds the Devil's death. The bell is tolled as many times as years have passed since Christ's birth in Bethlehem. It stops during the midnight service, and is then resumed until the total number is reached.

Maypole dancing takes place every third year at Barwick-in-Elmet, on Easter Monday and Whit Tuesday. In the presence of hundreds of spectators the village's famous 86ft maypole is uprooted and lowered for renewal. It is a difficult task as it weighs 55cwts. Several teams of village men are used for the lowering, and a bucketful of free beer is provided for their refreshment. During the following weeks the pole is painted and renovated, and the village women make thousands of rosettes for the traditional pole-raising and gala when there is a display of maypole dancing and the crowning of the Maypole Queen.

Midgley has its "Pace-Egg Play", which is performed round the village during the morning and afternoon on Good Friday. It is similar to the performances of the Christmas mummers, and its theme is the struggle between good and evil. The hero St. George fights the Black Prince of Paradine, Bold Slasher, Hector and other villians. The traditional doctor patches up the wounded players. The script goes back to the eighteenth century, although there are much older versions.

The industrial city of Sheffield keeps up the ancient custom of long-sword dancing. This takes place every Boxing Day in the suburbs of Grenoside outside the *Harrow Inn,* and the dancers then go to Handsworth where they finish up at the church.